Riverdale Cookbook

The Chock'lit Kitchen

By - Rene Reed

License Notes

Table of Contents

Introduction

Do you love Riverdale? Are you a fan of Archie comics and characters? Do you wish to throw the ultimate Riverdale themed party? You have come to the right place!

Riverdale is a show that gives us a glimpse into the dark side of the fictional town made popular by Archie comics.

It's a town that houses Riverdale high, a high school that stays in the limelight for its controversial on-goings.

But that's not what this book is about. It's to help you cook delicious dishes for your guests. These are inspired by Riverdale and come with a sample of the scene where the dishes appear.

The gang loves to hang out at Pop Tate's Chock'lit Shoppe, a diner that serves delicious food.

I hope you enjoy trying out these recipes.

Chapter 1: Drinks to Get the Party Started!

Strawberry Milkshake

Milkshakes are probably one of the most popular drinks on the show. They are a speciality at Pop Tates.

Serving size: 4

Cooking time: 5 minutes

Ingredients:

- ½ lb strawberries, chopped
- 2 tablespoons sugar
- 1 teaspoon vanilla extract
- 4 scoops vanilla ice cream
- ½ cup milk

Instructions:

Add strawberries, sugar, milk, vanilla ice cream and extract and to a blender and whizz.

Serve and enjoy!

Coffee

Literally, everybody on the show drinks coffee at one point or another. It is particularly popular with Veronica and Betty.

Serving size: 4

Cooking time: 30 minutes

Ingredients:

- 2 teaspoons instant coffee
- ½ cup milk
- ½ cup water
- 2 teaspoons sugar
- 1 teaspoon cinnamon
- 1 teaspoon cocoa powder

Instructions:

Add coffee and sugar to a cup and mix.

Add a little water to make a paste.

Boil milk and pour it into the coffee mixture and stir till combined.

Sprinkle cinnamon and cocoa powder over it and serve.

Smoothie

KJ Apa, who plays Archie on the show, once said that the milkshakes shown on the show are actually smoothies made using low-calorie yogurt.

Serving size: 2-3

Cooking time: 5 minutes

Ingredients:

- 2 cups bananas, sliced
- ½ cup yogurt
- ½ tablespoons flax seeds
- 1 cup almond milk
- 1 teaspoon vanilla extract

Instructions:

Add bananas, yogurt, flax seeds, almond milk and vanilla extract to a blender and whizz till smooth.

Add ice cubes and serve.

Ice Cream Soda

Ice cream sodas are always present on the table when the gang meets up at Pop Tates. They are just as popular in the comic and consumed very often.

Serving size: 1

Cooking time: 5 minutes

Ingredients:

- 1 tablespoon vanilla syrup
- ¼ cup vanilla ice cream
- ¼ cup milk
- 1 cup soda

Instructions:

Add the syrup and milk to a glass and mix.

Add the ice cream and pour the soda over it.

Cosmopolitan

If you thought I was going to mention only milkshakes and floats, then you are wrong! How can we leave out Veronica's favorite drink?

Serving size: 1

Cooking time: 5 minutes

Ingredients:

- 2 ounces orange vodka
- 1-ounce cranberry juice
- ½ ounce lime juice
- 1-ounce Cointreau
- Lime to garnish
- Ice cubes

Instructions:

Add vodka, lime juice, Cointreau, ice cubes and cranberry juice to a cocktail shaker and shake till combined.

Strain and serve with a lime wedge.

Shandy

All the dads on the show love beer. Be it Archie's, Jughead's, or the rest of the men from Southside Serpents, beer is widely seen on the show.

Serving size: 4

Cooking time: 5 minutes

Ingredients:

- 1 bottle lager beer
- ½ cup lemonade

Instructions:

Add the lemonade to a glass and pour the beer.

Mix and serve.

Chapter 2: Starters and Main Course

Onion Rings

The first time Archie and Veronica meet at Pop Tate's, Archie recommends she try the onion rings.

Serving size: 4

Cooking time: 30 minutes

Ingredients:

- 1 onion, sliced into circles
- 1 ¼ cups flour
- 1 teaspoon salt
- 1 teaspoon baking soda
- 1 egg
- 1 cup milk
- 1 cup breadcrumbs
- Salt to taste
- Oil to fry

Instructions:

Heat oil in a pot.

Add flour, baking powder, salt to a plate and mix.

Add the egg, milk and salt to a bowl and combine.

Spread the breadcrumbs on a plate.

Roll the onions in the flour and dunk them in the egg mixture.

Roll in the breadcrumbs and fry until golden brown.

Serve warm.

Cheeseburgers

One of the most eaten foods in Riverdale is the cheeseburger. Pop Tate's makes a delicious looking, tall burger.

Serving size: 4

Cooking time: 30 minutes

Ingredients:

- 2 lb beef, minced
- 1 tablespoon onion powder
- 10 cheese slices
- 5 burger buns
- Salt and pepper to taste

Instructions:

Add beef, onion, pepper and salt to a bowl and mix till combined.

Divide it into 5 patties and grill till crispy on both sides.

Place a cheese between the buns and a patty over it.

Add another slice on top and serve.

Roast Turkey

Before Hermione married Hiram, she was Fred's girlfriend. She waitressed at Pop Tate's and fell for Fred, who frequented the do. When they decide to get back together, she remembers his favorite order, "Turkey on rye, hold the tomatoes".

Serving size: 4-6

Cooking time: 45 minutes

Ingredients:

- 12 lb turkey
- 1 tablespoon garlic, minced
- 3 whole lemons, halved
- 5 thyme sprigs
- 6 rosemary sprigs
- Herb butter
- ½ cup oil
- 4 ounces butter
- 1 teaspoon thyme leaves
- 4 teaspoons garlic, minced
- Salt and pepper to taste

Instructions:

Add the turkey to a tray and stuff the cavity with garlic, lemon, thyme and rosemary.

Add the oil, butter, garlic, thyme, salt and pepper to a bowl and mix.

Rub it over the turkey.

Roast in a preheated 350 Fahrenheit oven for an hour.

Crank up the heat to 415 to make the skin crispy.

Serve warm.

Rye Bread

Rye bread is easy to make. You don't have to rush to the store to buy it and make a batch for your guests in the convenience of your kitchen.

Serving size: 4-6

Cooking time: 1 hour

Ingredients:

- 2/3 cup warm water
- ¼ cup oil
- ¾ cup pickle juice
- Salt and sugar to taste
- 2 teaspoons caraway seeds
- 2 teaspoons dill seeds
- 1 tablespoon mustard seeds
- ¾ cups potato flour
- 2 ½ cups bread flour
- 1 ¼ cup pumpernickel flour

Instructions:

Add the potato and pumpernickel flour to a bowl and mix.

Add salt, sugar, caraway, dill and mustard seeds and combine.

Add the water, oil, pickle juice to a bowl and mix.

Add to the flour mixture and make a firm dough and rest for 30 minutes.

Punch it and knead for 2 minutes.

Add the dough to a greased tin and bake in a preheated 350 Fahrenheit oven for 2 hours.

Slice and serve.

Cherry Tomato Salad

Fred might not like tomatoes in his sandwich, but your guests will surely fall for this delicious cherry tomato salad.

Serving size: 4

Cooking time: 15 minutes

Ingredients:

- 2 cups cherry tomatoes, halved
- 1 cup green olives, halved
- 5 ounces black olives, halved
- ½ cup olive oil
- 2 tablespoons wine vinegar
- 1 teaspoon sugar
- 1 teaspoon oregano
- 2 onions, finely chopped
- 4 ounces pine nuts
- Salt and pepper to taste

Instructions:

Add tomatoes, green and black olives and onion to a bowl and mix.

Add the nuts to a pan and brown.

Add it over the salad and toss.

Add oil, vinegar, sugar, oregano, salt and pepper to a small bowl and mix.

Drizzle it over the salad and serve.

Fries

If there is one thing other than cheeseburgers that are widely consumed by the characters, yes, fries.

Serving size: 4

Cooking time: 30 minutes

Ingredients:

- 3 medium-sized potatoes, cut into strips
- 4 cups cold water
- 1 tablespoon herbs-rosemary, oregano, thyme and parsley
- Salt and paprika to sprinkle
- Oil to fry

Instructions:

Soak the potato strips in cold water for 30 minutes.

Place them over tissues to soak the excess and pat them dry.

Add the oil to a deep pot and heat.

Gently lower the potato strips into the pot.

Make sure you don’t over crowd the pot.

Fry till golden and drain on tissues.

Add to a bowl and sprinkle the herbs, salt and paprika and shake.

Serve and enjoy.

Smoked Salmon Omelets

It's no secret that Veronica eats breakfast like a queen. She enjoys delicious eggs at home while checking her phone for the latest gossip in Riverdale High. Here is a recipe she would surely enjoy.

Serving size: 4

Cooking time: 30 minutes

Ingredients:

- 1 tablespoon oil
- ¼ lb zucchini, grated
- 3 spring onions, chopped
- Salt and pepper to taste
- 4 eggs
- 2 tablespoons cream cheese
- 1 tablespoon butter
- 1 salmon, slit and chopped

Instructions:

Heat oil and sauté the onions and zucchini till golden.

Add eggs and cream to a bowl and mix till combined.

Pour it into a warm saucepan along with butter and swirl it around.

Sprinkle the salmon over it.

Add to a plate and serve with salt and pepper.

Orange Salad

Veronica always has a glass of orange juice next to her breakfast plate. But it would be quite boring to serve guests' plain orange juice. Here is a delicious orange salad recipe that you and your guests will savor.

Serving size: 4

Cooking time: 30 minutes

Ingredients:

- 1 onion, sliced (refrigerate for an hour)
- 12 mint leaves, chopped
- 1 orange, peeled
- Salt and paprika to taste
- 1 teaspoon cinnamon powder
- 1 pomegranate
- For dressing
- 1 lemon, juiced
- 1 tablespoon olive oil
- 1 tablespoon honey
- 2 teaspoons orange blossom water

Instructions:

Add lemon juice, oil, honey and orange blossom water to a bowl and mix till combined.

Arrange the onion slices on a large platter followed by orange slices and sprinkle mint, salt, pepper and paprika over it.

Sprinkle pomegranate and drizzle the dressing on top.

Serve and enjoy.

Tomato Avocado Toast

Another popular item on the menu at the Lodge household is tomato on toast. To up the flavor profile, here is a tomato and avocado toast to try out.

Serving size: 4

Cooking time: 45 minutes

Ingredients:

- 1 baguette
- 2 tablespoons oil
- 1 avocado, scooped
- 1 teaspoon lemon juice
- Cherry tomatoes, halved
- Salt and pepper to taste

Instructions:

Slice the baguette in half and toast the inner side.

Add the avocado to a bowl along with the lemon, salt and pepper and mix.

Toss in the tomatoes and combine.

Apply it over the toast and serve.

Hot Dog

There are two foods that we normally associate with Jughead. One being burgers and the other being hotdogs. Hot dog is Jughead's naughty pooch.

Serving size: 4

Cooking time: 30 minutes

Ingredients:

- 2 tablespoons cheddar cheese, grated
- 3 teaspoons mustard
- 1 tablespoon honey
- 4 sausages
- 4 brioche buns

Instructions:

Add the cheese, honey and mustard to a bowl and mix.

Grill the sausages on all sides.

Slice open the buns and add a sausage in between.

Sprinkle the cheese over it and serve.

Subway

Although Jughead is often seen having burgers, I'm sure he also enjoys subs!

Serving size: 4

Cooking time: 30 minutes

Ingredients:

- Baguette
- 4 cheese slices
- 6 turkey slices
- 1 tomato, sliced
- 6 lettuce leaves
- 5 cucumber slices
- 1 green pepper, sliced
- Olives
- Jalapeños
- 2 tablespoons mayonnaise
- 1 tablespoon sweet onion sauce

Instructions:

Add the bread to a cutting board and slice in half.

Toast the bread on the inner side and add meat slices.

Follow it with lettuce leaves and tomato slices.

Add cucumber and bell pepper slices along with olives and jalapeños.

Drizzle mayonnaise and hot sauce over it and finish it with cheese slices.

Serve and enjoy!

Lobster Bisque

When Veronica invites Archie over for dinner and introduces him to her parents, an exquisite dinner is laid out on the table. One of the first things served is a lobster bisque.

Serving size: 4

Cooking time: 30 minutes

Ingredients:

- 3 lobster tails
- 1 tablespoon oil
- 1 tablespoon garlic, minced
- 2 tablespoons chickpea flour/regular flour
- ½ teaspoon hot sauce
- ¼ cup vinegar
- Salt and pepper to taste
- 1 teaspoon thyme
- 1/3 cup chicken broth
- 2/3 cup tomato puree
- 1 teaspoon paprika
- 2 cups lobster base
- 1 cup coconut milk
- 2 shallots, chopped

Instructions:

Boil a pot of water and add the lobster tails and cook for 10 minutes.

Remove the lobster and reserve the water.

Once the lobsters cool, gently remove the shells and scoop out the flesh into a bowl.

Add the shells back to the water and boil for 10 minutes.

Add oil to a pan and toss in the garlic and shallots to brown for 5 minutes.

Stir in the chickpea flour and pour wine into the pan to deglaze.

Add hot sauce, salt, pepper and thyme and simmer till thick.

Pour the chicken broth and half the lobster water and boil.

Add tomato and paprika and mix.

Allow the mixer to cool before blending it till smooth or use an immersion blender to do so.

Add it back to the pan and toss in the lobster meat along with coconut milk and boil for 5 minutes.

Serve warm and enjoy.

Pancakes

Veronica walks into The Choklit Shoppe and greets a waiting Jughead. She notices her foundation is out of place, so she grabs a pancake and fixes it.

Serving size: 4

Cooking time: 30 minutes

Ingredients:

- 1 cup flour
- 2 teaspoons baking powder
- ½ teaspoon salt
- Pepper to taste
- 1 cup milk
- 2 tablespoons butter
- 1 egg
- 1 tablespoon oil

Instructions:

Add flour, baking powder, salt, pepper, milk, egg, butter to a bowl and mix until well combined.

Add oil to a griddle and a ladleful of the mixture.

Flip the pancake once it turns brown and cook the other side.

Serve warm with curry.

Pizza

Archie and Jughead enjoy a pizza and a beer when they catch up with each other in Archie's house.

Serving size: 4

Cooking time: 30 minutes

Ingredients:

- 1 pizza base
- 1 cup marinara sauce
- 2 cups spinach
- 3 cups mozzarella cheese, grated
- ½ cup artichoke, chopped
- ½ cup bell pepper, chopped
- 1 onion, sliced
- ½ cup cherry tomatoes, halved
- ½ cup olives, halved
- ½ cup chicken, cooked and chopped
- Basil leaves

Instructions:

Add the pizza base to a tray and apply sauce over it.

Sprinkle tomato, spinach, basil, artichoke, pepper, onion, olives and chicken over it, followed by the cheese and roast in a preheated 500 Fahrenheit oven for 30 minutes.

Slice and enjoy.

BLT

The Chock'lit Shoppe offers a delicious BLT sandwich that Jughead absolutely loves.

Serving size: 1

Cooking time: 30 minutes

Ingredients:

- 4 bacon slices
- 2 tablespoons chives, chopped
- 1 teaspoon lemon juice
- Mayonnaise
- 2 burger buns or bread slices
- 2 lettuce leaves
- 1 tomato, sliced
- Salt and pepper

Instructions:

Heat a grill and grill the bacon slices.

Add mayonnaise, lemon juice and chives to a bowl and whisk.

Slice the buns and apply the mayonnaise.

Add the lettuce leaves and tomato followed by the bacon.

Sprinkle salt and pepper to taste.

Cover and enjoy.

Veggie Burger

Pretty sure not everyone on the show eats meat and there are some who prefer veg options. Pop Tate's surely offers a veg burger at his diner.

Serving size: 4

Cooking time: 30 minutes

Ingredients:

- 1 cup black beans
- 3 tablespoons tomato ketchup
- Salt to taste
- 1 teaspoon garlic, minced
- 1 onion, chopped
- 2 tablespoons flour
- 1 cup vegetables-beans, carrots, peas, potatoes, chopped
- Burger buns

Instructions:

Cook the beans and vegetables till they reach a mash-able consistency.

Add to a bowl along with onion, garlic, salt and flour and mix.

Add a little oil to a hot skillet.

Divide the mixture into 4-5 patties and roast until golden on both sides.

Slice the buns open and apply ketchup.

Add a patty in between and serve.

Bagels

The breakfast menu at Chock'lit Shoppe has bagels listed on it. Although the characters mostly prefer scrambled eggs, I'm sure the bagels are delicious too.

Serving size: 4

Cooking time: 30 minutes

Ingredients:

- 1 ¼ cups water
- 4 ½ cups flour
- 3 tablespoons sugar
- 1 teaspoon salt or to taste
- 2 tablespoons oil
- 1 tablespoon yeast
- 4 quarts water
- Sesame seeds to sprinkle

Instructions:

Add water, flour, sugar, salt, oil and yeast to a bowl and combine.

It should come together into a smooth dough.

Apply oil to the dough and rest for 2 hours.

Punch the dough and divide it into 6 pieces.

Roll the pieces into oblongs and join the two ends together.

Place them over a lined or greased baking tray and sprinkle sesame seeds over each.

Bake in a preheated 475 Fahrenheit oven for 20 to 30 minutes.

Serve and enjoy.

Bowl of Salad

Mrs. Cooper serves a big bowl of salad to Betty.

Serving size: 4

Cooking time: 20 minutes

Ingredients:

- 5 ounces spring greens
- 1 cucumber, sliced
- ½ cup pine nuts, toasted
- 1 onion, sliced
- For dressing
- 3 tablespoons oil
- 1 tablespoon lemon juice
- 1 teaspoon mustard
- 1 teaspoon garlic, minced
- Salt and pepper to taste

Instructions:

Add oil, lemon juice, mustard, garlic, salt and pepper to a bowl and whisk.

Add greens, cucumber, onion and pine nuts to a large bowl and toss.

Drizzle the dressing and serve.

Chapter 3: Desserts

Doughnuts

Doughnuts are widely consumed on the show. Chocolate, white cream, strawberry, there are many to choose from!

Serving size: 4

Cooking time: 30 minutes

Ingredients:

- 2 tablespoons shortening
- ½ cup sugar
- 1 egg
- ½ teaspoon vanilla extract
- 2 cups flour
- ½ teaspoon baking soda
- Oil to fry
- 2 tablespoons vinegar
- 3/8 cup milk

Confectioners sugar to sprinkle

Instructions:

Add milk and vinegar to a bowl and allow it to curdle.

Add shortening, sugar. Soda, flour and salt to a bowl and combine.

Pour the milk mixture into the flour and make a dough.

Turn it on to a floured surface and knead till soft.

Divide it into 6 to 7 rolls and roll into oblongs.

Join the two ends to make doughnut shapes.

Heat oil in a pan and fry doughnuts till golden.

Drain on tissues and sprinkle confectioner's sugar over it.

Serve and enjoy.

Ice Cream Sundae

Ice cream sundaes are widely enjoyed on the show. From Betty to Veronica to Jughead to Archie to Cheryl, everyone loves them!

Serving size: 4

Cooking time: 30 minutes

Ingredients:

- 1 cup pineapple, sliced
- ¼ cup coconut liqueur
- 1 tablespoon caster sugar
- Desiccated coconut, to sprinkle
- 4 ginger biscuits, crumbled
- 4 ice cream scoops (flavor of your choice)

Instructions:

Add pineapple, liqueur and sugar to a pan and brown.

Crumble the biscuits and add them to serving bowls.

Add ice cream scoops into each bowl and drizzle the liqueur mixture over it.

Sprinkle coconut and serve.

Cake

As we know, Jughead loves to eat heartily. He uses his bare hands to dig into a cake and gobbles it up.

Serving size: 4

Cooking time: 30 minutes

Ingredients:

- 2 cups flour
- 4 eggs
- 1 cup sugar
- ¾ cup oil
- ½ cup milk
- 1 teaspoon vanilla extract
- 2 teaspoons baking powder

Instructions:

Add flour and baking powder to a bowl and whisk.

Add sugar and oil to a bowl and whisk till fluffy.

Add vanilla and combine.

Separate the eggs and beat the whites till stiff peaks form.

Add egg yolks to the sugar mixture and beat.

Mix the sugar and flour mixture and combine.

Fold in the egg whites and transfer to a greased tray.

Bake in a preheated 350 Fahrenheit oven for 35 minutes.

Slice and enjoy.

Waffles

Waffles are a popular dessert in most of the characters' houses and are often ordered at the Chock'lit Shoppe.

Serving size: 4

Cooking time: 30 minutes

Ingredients:

- 1 cup flour
- 2 tablespoons sugar
- 1 teaspoon baking powder
- ¼ teaspoon salt
- 1 cup milk
- 2 eggs
- 4 tablespoons butter
- Honey to drizzle

Instructions:

Add flour, baking powder and salt to a bowl and combine.

Add milk, eggs and sugar and make a smooth batter.

Grease the waffle pan with butter and add a ladleful of the mixture.

Add prepared waffles to a plate and drizzle honey over it.

Macarons

The girls on the show love macaroons. Be it pink, green, yellow, or white; they love biting into the colorful little macarons.

Serving size: 4

Cooking time: 45 minutes

Ingredients:

- 1 cup powdered sugar
- ½ cup almond flour
- 3 egg whites
- 3 tablespoons sugar to sprinkle
- Food colour-green, yellow, pink
- Flavor
- 1 cup buttercream

Instructions:

Add sugar and flour in a processor and mix till combined.

Add egg whites to a bowl and whip till stiff peaks form.

Gently add a tablespoon of the sugar at a time.

Reduce the speed to low and add the flavor.

Ad into piping bags and make circles on a lined tray.

Bake in a preheated 325 Fahrenheit oven for 10 minutes and cool.

Beat the cream till fluffy.

Divide it into bowls and add a color into each and mix.

Spoon or pipe the buttercream between the biscuits and sandwich them.

Rainbow Cupcakes

Here are cupcakes to celebrate the character of Kevin Keller.

Serving size: 4

Cooking time: 30 minutes

Ingredients:

- 3 1/4 cups flour
- 2 ½ teaspoons baking powder
- 1 cup butter, softened
- 2 cups sugar
- 2 eggs
- 2 teaspoons vanilla extract
- 1 ½ cups milk
- Buttercream, as desire
- Colorful sprinkles, as desire

Instructions:

Add flour and baking powder to a bowl and whisk.

Add sugar and butter and cream.

Add vanilla extract and mix.

Add the eggs and beat till combined.

Add the flour into the wet mixture and combine till a smooth batter.

Add the mixture into cupcake molds and bake in a preheated 350 Fahrenheit oven for 20 minutes.

Cool the cupcakes.

Beat the buttercream till fluffy.

Add to piping bag and pipe over the cupcakes.

Sprinkle the rainbow sprinkles and serve.

Conclusion

Thank you for choosing this book and I hope you had fun reading it.

Riverdale is an interesting show and so is the food showcased in it.

You and your guests will have a great time trying out these recipes. Feel free to give them your spin and come up with unique dishes.

Bon Appetit!

About the Author

Contemporary Caribbean cuisine had never tasted so good before Rene Reed came into the scene. With about twenty years dedicated to building up a budding culinary career, Rene has worked in various top-end restaurants, hotels, and resorts as the head chef. Her dive into the food industry started in Michigan, where she trained with some of the best chefs on the block. Rene was an accountant at a top firm but didn't feel a sense of accomplishment at the end of the day. Something was missing, and although Rene didn't know it at that time, the answer was right under her nose.

She discovered how relaxed and happy she felt when she was trying to whip up something in the kitchen for her family. To her, cooking was equivalent to vacation time, where she could do whatever she wanted. Encouraged by her family and loved ones, Rene quit her job and started her culinary training in earnest. Her efforts yielded so much success as she built up a network that propelled her to key positions all around the industry.

She specializes in exceptional Caribbean cuisine while also adding that unique Rene touch to every menu as much as she can.

Author's Afterthoughts

Thank you for taking out time to read my work. I put in all those hours, and I'm super glad that you found it worthy enough to download. I would love to ask for one more thing, and that is your feedback. It will be lovely to know your thoughts on the contents of the book. Was it worth your time? Would you like me to change anything for my subsequent books? I'll love to hear them all.

Thanks!

Rene Reed

Made in the USA
Middletown, DE
03 October 2022

11803059R00044